SOCIAL MEDIA MARKETING FOR BUSINESS 2020::

The Ultimate Mastery Workbook for Beginners to Create a Brand and Become a Skilled Influencer: Personal Branding & Digital Networking Strategies.

KIM MILLUCCI

© Copyright 2020 - All rights reserved.

The content contained within this book may not be reproduced, duplicated or transmitted without direct written permission from the author or the publisher.

Under no circumstances will any blame or legal responsibility be held against the publisher, or author, for any damages, reparation, or monetary loss due to the information contained within this book. Either directly or indirectly.

Legal Notice:

This book is copyright protected. This book is only for personal use. You cannot amend, distribute, sell, use, quote or paraphrase any part, or the content within this book, without the consent of the author or publisher.

Disclaimer Notice:

Please note the information contained within this document is for educational and entertainment purposes only. All effort has been executed to present accurate, up to date, and reliable, complete information. No warranties of any kind are declared or implied. Readers acknowledge that the author is not engaging in the rendering of legal, financial, medical or professional advice. The content within this book has been derived from various sources. Please consult a licensed professional before attempting any techniques outlined in this book.

By reading this document, the reader agrees that under no circumstances is the author responsible for any losses, direct or indirect, which are incurred as a result of the use of information contained within this document, including, but not limited to, — errors, omissions, or inaccuracies.

Table Of Contents

Introduction 3

Chapter 1: Understanding Social Media Marketing? 6

Chapter 2: Social Media Marketing For Businesses 13

Chapter 3: How To Build Your Brand? 21

Chapter 4: Creating A Social Media Marketing Strategy 28

Chapter 5: Prioritizing The Top Platform For Your Brand................................ 30

Chapter 6: Twitter Marketing 36

Chapter 7: Facebook Marketing 38

Chapter 8: Youtube Marketing 45

Chapter 9: Instagram Marketing..51

Chapter 10: Benefits Of Social Media Marketing 56

Chapter 11: Measuring Your Marketing Success 61

Chapter 12: Why Do People Fail At Social Media Marketing? 63

Chapter 13: Search Engine Optimization & Social Media Marketing 69

Chapter 14: How To Build Your Brand's Awareness And Deliver Top Customer Service 71

Chapter 15: Simple & Effective Outsourcing To Build Your Social Media Team 77

Chapter 16: Planning Your Social Media Marketing Content 79

Chapter 17: Tips And Tricks To Social Media Marketing Success In 2020 81

Chapter 18: Government Regulation For Social Media Marketing 83

Conclusion 85

Introduction

Before embarking on the social media marketing journey, you need to know what social media marketing is, including the history of the concept and how it evolved to become a much-needed tool in your business. You will learn these answers, as well as what social media does for your audience, the key advantages and potential disadvantages to you and your audience in this guide

As you read the pages, you will discover the value of branding your company and how to ensure your brand is successful with the critical rules of a good brand.

Once you have the starting foundation, you will launch into individual social media sites, their history, tips, and steps to set up an account with these sites. Each chapter has vital information to help you get started.

This book will not discuss content marketing with any depth. It will mention the content, grammar, and consistency of posts; however, a full discussion of content is not included. Content marketing is a massive topic on its own.

Social media marketing is taking some local small businesses from the ground up to have very successful businesses with consistent growth. Those results are not typical for every local small business, but it's fascinating for many reasons which we will discuss later.

The information in this book will help you to create and grow a strong social media presence for your business that will allow you to obtain all the potential that social media has to offer.

For many business owners, the idea of increasing revenue through social media marketing efforts sounds farfetched. Some find it daunting, especially when they consider the big brands in their space that have amassed large followings and invest millions of dollars each year into marketing. When you feel like a grasshopper, it can seem impossible to compete against the giants of the land. But here's the thing on social media, the grasshopper has an even higher chance of winning real business than the giant. Why?

All you need to do is understand the game of winning on social media. By reading this specific book, you've just increased the chances of blowing up your business growth in unimaginable ways. You are, in essence, taking a step in the direction of more business growth, freedom, and financial prosperity simply because all the attention and eyeballs reside on social media.

This level of change makes it difficult to pin down what needs to be done to stay up to date with social media marketing, especially for those who are still getting the hang of the entire process in the first place. Anything is not impossible, however, which is why the following chapters will discuss everything you need to know to get started building a social media marketing plan that you can be relatively confident will last for years to come with minimal alterations.

The world of social media moves incredibly fast. Search engines and social networks continuously change the rules of the game, and tactics and strategies change to keep up with the new rules. It can be overwhelming to stay on top of all of these changes on all of the social networks, all the time. But no matter how quickly things change, the basics remain the same. This book is focused on the basics of the social media marketing that will teach you how to adapt to every change that will happen in the future. If you stick to the basics, the rest is easy.

KIM MILLUCCI

Let's dive in!

Chapter 1: Understanding Social Media Marketing?

Social media marketing is a way of gaining traffic to your website through the use of social media sites. Marketing efforts in this area tend to concentrate on creating content that attracts the attention of their chosen audience and encouraging them to share it with all their friends and followers across social media. The result is an electronic word of mouth that spreads fast, earning the marketer good media visibility for next to no outlay.

The internet has become the main focus of all marketers. Print and TV advertisements now point to the website and social accounts of the company. The entire marketing campaign for any company, no matter how big or small, is tied around the company's web presence. But why is this so?

Just think about how many people are connected to the internet today. Almost the entire consumer base is present online, and it spends a lot of time online. The mobile phone revolution shrunk the entire world into a globalized society, and the advent of smartphones has connected the whole world by bringing the internet in the palms of our hands. There are more than a billion users just on Facebook.

The numbers alone are baffling but now think about what these people do on the internet. They connect with family, friends, strangers, and colleagues, and they talk about their lives. They share jokes, news, photographs, and videos. And they talk about products. Every marketer will tell you that the best type of marketing is "word of mouth" marketing.

When you hear about a product from someone you know, you automatically have more trust than if you were watching an advertisement on television. Social media marketing results in this type of word of mouth publicity that has a much more significant impact on prospective consumers than any other form of marketing. It also has the possibility of growing exponentially by going viral.

We've all heard about viral videos that reached millions of viewers in a few days. This potential to go viral is also why all marketers now focus on a lot of social media. And on top of all that, it's one of the cheapest forms of marketing. Social media websites work by letting people interact with each other and build up relationships. When a business joins in, it allows potential customers to interact directly with them, creating a more personal touch and ensuring that customers are likely to pass the word about you on to their friends and families. And, because they are sharing your news with their friends, more people get to see it and pass it on to their friends, and so on, resulting in an increase in traffic that may convert to sales.

Social media marketing is used by more than 70% of today's businesses and has resulted in an increase of more than 130% in revenue. It isn't only computers that are used for surfing the internet; mobile phones and tablets are now used much more for accessing social media websites than they ever have been. Most smartphones have social media apps enabled, and people are notified immediately when anything happens on their social media sites. This is a constant connection that allows businesses to keep their customers fully in the loop about what's happening and what's new.

As you plan your social media marketing strategy, you need to look at all of the platforms available. What is the popularity like, what marketing opportunities are there, what type of content will you need to create and share, and do you have the right content that will be engaging enough to generate leads and purchases? Taking advantage of every social media platform available to you may be the best option for you and your company, or it may be beneficial just to use one or two platforms.

Social Media Marketing Strategy

Your social media marketing strategy should identify your business goals. You need to have a clear vision of what you are working towards so that you can create objectives to attain them. Your goals may be to increase brand awareness, retain your customers, introduce new products or services, expand to a new geographic or demographic market, etc. Choose two or three primary goals that you believe are attainable from your list, as well as two or three secondary goals that you want to focus on in this marketing strategy.

Once you have your goals clearly defined, you can then develop specific measures to achieve those goals. Ask yourself how you can meet those goals. If one of your primary goals is to increase brand awareness, what can you feasibly do to achieve that goal? Use Facebook advertising and contests? Generate Twitter posts on a routine basis? Whatever the objectives are, you should be able to meet the goal successfully promptly. Your goals should be specific, measurable, achievable, relevant, and time-bound. Note: Do not overshoot your goals. For example, do not set a goal that you will reach over one million users on social media within the first year. This is highly unfeasible and unrealistic. Make sure your goals are relevant and consistent with your company's mission.

Using social media as a marketing tool is a great way to heighten your brand awareness and tap into new users, especially the younger market. However, social media marketing is a longterm goal and takes a lot of time and effort to achieve a high standing status. Be patient with your goals and reassess what they mean to you and your company monthly, if not weekly.

Now that you know your audience, what does your competition look like? Take an active approach in studying your competition to understand what social media platforms they are currently using and what type of content seems to attract the most response. You can use these notes as you decide what social media platforms you believe will be the most beneficial for you and the kind of content you need to post to be successful. The most important thing you need to remember is that engagement is your number one goal. If you are posting daily on any social media platform, or perhaps all of them, but are not getting any engagement, or very little, it's time to rethink your plans. Go over your goals, see what others are doing, and restart your social media marketing.

Once you find out what seems to be working for your competitors and you have done your research to determine what will work best for your business (remember your research should be based on your goals and objectives as well what works for your competitors), it is time to decide what social media platforms you will use. I will tell you that most people spend at least 40% of their online time on Facebook and at least 20% of their time on Twitter. These two platforms are almost a given for any new social media marketing campaign.

You can also use one form of social media more frequently than the other. Say, for example, you focus more energy on Facebook, and post a little less on Twitter. You're still reaching an audience and putting your name out there, but you are focusing your efforts on one social media platform more than you are in another. You can also increase the time and money spent on other platforms as you continue to grow and feel comfortable using social media for marketing. A simple way to even out the amount of time you are spending on your platforms is to link your accounts. For instance, you can link your Facebook and Twitter accounts, so that when you post something on one, it will automatically post to the other.

Once you have settled on your social media platforms, you need to develop your content strategy. Content is significant in building relationships online. Your new accounts will be meaningless unless you have meaningful content to connect you with new followers (either current customers or prospective customers). Your content strategy will include what content you will post, the timing of your posts, and the frequency you should be posting. Different types of content can be posted: pure text, images, links, video, etc. All of these have their value, which will be discussed later on.

Now that the entire social media marketing strategy has been written, it is time to allocate some time and resources to this plan. You need to decide how much money you are willing to assign to the social media side of advertising as opposed to traditional advertising.

This entire process should be a work in process as you build your social media marketing strategy. Ultimately, it will be as successful as you make it. This book is designed to give you the tools you need to make each social media platform as successful as possible.

What Can You Do with Social Media?

If you have an online presence and are active on a few social networks and have a quality audience, you can do the following:

Sell your products to your audience.

This is the primary goal of any type of marketing. When you sell to a handpicked audience, all of whom have shown an interest in your product, the chances of making a sale increase a lot. All other forms of advertising are intrusive and force themselves on the audience. You sit down to watch your favorite movie, and someone interrupts you and tries to sell you something.

Ask your audience to help you spread the word.

This is possible only with social media marketing, and if you have developed strong relationships with your audience, they won't mind doing this work for you at all. If your product has provided them value and you have shown that you listen to your audience, then they'll happily become missionaries for your product, spreading your name wherever they go.

Listen to your audience to help improve your products and services.

This is an immense value proposition of social media marketing. Usually, companies pay customers to participate in surveys so that they can develop better products. But on social media, you get constant feedback from your audience, and if used intelligently, it will help you offer the best value to your audience.

Provide excellent customer service to build a sharp brand image.

Social media is great for providing quick customer service to anyone who has a complaint or question. If done right, it will put you in a rare league of companies that care about their customers. Keep your customers happy, and they'll talk about you with their friends.

Allow your customers to help you develop your business.

It's called crowdfunding. If you have a secure connection with your audience, it can help you raise money without having to go to traditional sources for a loan. This is way beyond any kind of traditional marketing.

Standard Features of Social Media

What connects the different social media platforms? As a rule of thumb, they all contain several varying features that are differently presented from app to app; yet still familiar to most users. The three essential features are listed below.

- **Profile Page**: It's an essential part of a social media platform, as this is the user's way to create content and interact with others. It will usually feature a photo as well as a small description. The depth of these descriptions and profiles varies. Facebook has a relatively extended profile, featuring information about your education and family members and the like, while Instagram only allows you a 140character description below your name.

- **News Feed:** To see what your friends and your followed companies are posting, you'll have to check the newsfeed. Updated in realtime, your newsfeed features posts from peers and companies, which you can usually 'like,' comment on, or even share. While different outlets have different names for the posts, such as Twitter referencing a share as a "retweet," the fundamental idea is the same.

- **Hashtag:** While you can easily see your friends' content on your feeds, the hashtag allows users to connect their content globally with as little as a symbol "#." For example, if a user has a status update on a great meal at a specific restaurant, the user can create the status update and hashtag it with the brand name, **i.e.,** #DominosPizza or #McDonalds, thereby allowing other users to search the brand name and see the post. Hashtags have been one of the most effective ways to launch campaigns and connects users to a topic of discussion.

Chapter 2: Social Media Marketing for Businesses

Social media marketing is an essential pathway for all kinds of businesses to interact with customers and prospects. As it is, your customers are probably already interacting with other brands via popular social media sites. Therefore, you should also be speaking to them, posting content, and interacting on these social networking sites; otherwise, you will lose out.

Some of the more popular social websites include Instagram, Pinterest, Twitter, YouTube, Facebook, and Google. If you have an online business, make sure that you get it onto one or more of these platforms. Social media can bring you remarkable success and supply you with devoted brand advocates. You will also be able to handle additional matters via social media, including sales, customer services, and so on.

Social media marketing is a kind of internet marketing technique. It involves the creation of content and sharing it on social media platforms with friends, followers, and the general public. There are hundreds of millions of social media users around the world. Attracting them to your business via social media is essentially what social media marketing is all about.

Some everyday activities associated with social media marketing include posting relevant videos, uploading written posts, and updating images. You post all these to entice your viewers, readers, and followers. When you engage them, answer their questions, or respond to their comments, you gain credibility, and they begin to trust in you. Driving audience engagement and placing paid advertisements are also crucial aspects of social media marketing.

Marketing strategies for small businesses

A lot of small business owners are careful about where they spend their money. They choose carefully the marketing strategies that they invest in mostly because they have a limited budget and wish to get as much out of their investments as possible.

It is advisable as a small business owner to spend wisely to get the best returns. One of the most effective ways of doing this is marketing through social media platforms. This kind of approach is versatile with cost-effective strategies that work. It is no wonder that over 97% of all marketers use social media as most of their customers and potential customers are on one or more of these platforms.

Your customers are on social media

One of the reasons why you should market your small business is that your customers are on social media and spending considerable amounts of time each day. According to reliable statistics, over 70% of US residents are on one social media platform or other. The number of social media users around the world is expected to increase to about 2.5 billion this year. Since so many consumers are using social media, it only makes sense to reach out to them. Social media provides small businesses with an opportunity to reach out to a broad audience.

Consumers are more responsive to social media

It has been established that consumers are more receptive to marketing messages on social media than most other platforms. The reason is that social networking websites provide a fun and exciting way to interact, network, and keep in touch with friends and family. While users do not necessarily get online to receive marketing messages from businesses, they are very receptive, especially when approached engagingly and interactively. Most consumers on social media are happy to interact with their favourite brands.

Brand recognition on social media

One of the main benefits of social media is that it helps small business owners improve the visibility of their brands and products. When visibility is enhanced, your brand gets recognition and acceptance by your viewers and followers. You need to create business social media profiles across different platforms because these will open new doors and present new and exciting opportunities. You get to share content and also present your brand's personality and voice.

Build Your Brand

When you share content online, you get a fantastic opportunity to create an online persona. This persona generally reflects your professional skills as well as personal values. Many business owners use social media only as a platform to put out their brands and products. Many others gain useful connections, crucial leads, and eventually faithful followers and customers.

Product Launch on Social Media

The weeks and days leading up to product launch can be rather hectic and exciting at the same time. However, the most crucial part of a product launch should be getting the word out. Think about a tree that falls in the forest. Does it make a sound if no one is around? The same question applies to product launches, and this is where social media platforms come in handy. Social networks help to get the word out there.

Social media has completely altered the face of advertising. When used correctly, social media can help to boost a product. Social sites like Facebook and Instagram are excellent for product launches. There are reasons why such launches are so successful, and these reasons must be noted.

Build anticipation

Yet another crucial aspect of a product launch is building anticipation. This means throwing hints around, posting product images, and generally creating hype around the launch. This will create a buzz across different social media, and thousands of users will set the ball rolling by discussing the set launch as well as your brand and products. However, you need to be careful with an anticlimax release because these can hurt your brand. Also, ensure that you can handle a considerable demand once your product launches.

Word of mouth

One of the most effective methods of getting the word out and advertising a product is through word of mouth. Social media sites capitalize on this and help to get the word out there to hundreds of millions of people. As an online business owner, you need to be strategic with your approach.

Attract early adopters

It is advisable to attract early adopters to your products. Tech products are especially attractive to this breed of individuals. They love to be among the first to try out a new product in the market and then provide reviews on social media and weblogs. When you attract the early adopters, they will very shortly after that become your marketing champions well ahead of time. You should allow influencers a sneak peek at your products and let them leak the information to their thousands of online fans and followers. This will help create a viral buzz and hype the market, so they are eager to receive and use your products.

Targeting your market

One of the benefits of using social media is that there are settings that allow you to target a specific section of the market. It is a fact that most social media users are between the ages of 18 to 35. This age bracket is tremendously influential when it comes to the success of a newly launched product.

Social Media Marketing and Small Businesses and Franchises

Small businesses are often looking for new and effective ways of getting their businesses and brand out there so that potential customers can find them. If you are not already using social media, then you are losing out in a significant way. Social media is excellent for your business as it provides you with an avenue to attract new customers while engaging current ones regularly.

Small businesses have a huge advantage over large businesses when it comes to social media marketing. The reason is that to be effective, and you need to engage with followers, customers, and the general public. A business that does not engage with its followers and customers will not enjoy any success on social media.

How to Use Social Media for Franchises and Social Media

1. Begin with a modest focus: As a business owner seeking to attract new customers and an impressive following, you will probably get tempted to open up accounts on all known social media sites. However, you should hold back on this approach. Instead, open only one social media account and focus on it for a while. Only after you have learned the ropes can you proceed and open up additional accounts on other platforms.

2. Create a blog: One of the most useful platforms that can help with your social media marketing efforts is a blog. If you already have a website, then set up the blog is easy. However, it is advisable to have a separate website for your blog.

3. Create a content calendar: It is a great idea to plan your posts so that your engagements on social media are regular and coordinated rather than irregular and abrupt. You should try and plan your social engagements for at least one month in advance. In the meantime, you can always search other social networks or websites for suitable content to share with your followers. Try and engage them about four times each week or thereabouts.

4. Take the time to build an audience: It takes time and effort to build a reasonable following on social media. Most of your followers will only follow you if you invite them directly. Therefore, take the time to find followers and build an audience. Also, your followers will expect to receive fresh and engaging content every 3 to 4 days from you. It takes about six months for your followers to trust you and start buying your products. At that time, they will share your content with their networks and followers and also bombard you with questions about your products.

5. Measure your success: Once you start getting a sizable following on social media and conversion into leads and sales, you should start measuring the effectiveness and success of your efforts. What you need to do is to track results so that you find out how many of your new customers originate from social media sites. If they are engaging in social media, then you need to get in touch and find out more information about them. Tracking the performance of your social media is essential for your success.

6. Learn more about advertising before paying for it: Sometimes, it is necessary to advertise on social media. Paying for advertisements is advisable; however, do not just dive into it. Instead, take the time to learn about social media advertising. Also, ensure first that you have a sizable following before placing adverts. If you simply jump into advertising without careful planning and consideration, then you are very likely to lose money.

Reasons Why Small Businesses are More Successful on Social Media

1. They are focused more on communities and the individual: There are vast differences between small businesses and large corporations. For instance, large companies have vast numbers of employees, numerous legal and administrative structures with significant decisions being made at the headquarters far away. However, some differences are even more fundamental.

2. Social media advertising is very cost-effective: Conventional advertising is a costly affair. However, things are very different on social media because the costs are almost nonexistent. It is possible to conduct an entire campaign from launch to sales without spending any significant amount of money. Social media has hundreds of millions of users, so being able to reach this sizable population for only a fraction of the cost of conventional advertising is significant. And even when you decide to invest some resources into actual advertising on social media, you will be able to select your target audience, and the costs will remain low and affordable.

3. Joint social media marketing efforts: Sometimes, small businesses come together on social media to run joint campaigns. They collaborate in this manner to put their efforts towards similar social media marketing strategies. It is sometimes an excellent idea as a local business to partner with other businesses within the same local area, to send messages to customers within a particular niche. Keep in mind that these are not competitors but businesses that share the same interests and selling in the same neighborhood.

4. Personalized attention to customers: Small businesses love to pay personalized attention to their customers. For many consumers, shopping at a small business provides them with an excellent experience. A majority of consumers love to shop at local stores because they receive personalized attention. As a business owner, you should take your time to connect with your customers on an individual basis.

5. Small businesses can take advantage of prominent advertising: There are certain large marketing and advertising events held occasionally. Small businesses can leverage these events into their social marketing strategies. Take, for instance, the Small Business Saturday or SBS. This is a day set aside to celebrate and promote small businesses across America. It takes place on Saturday following Thanksgiving. Since plenty of consumers are aware of this day, you can leverage by promoting your products and maybe giving discounts to encourage customers to buy your products or use your services. This gives you a massive opportunity to gain customers and make sales.

Remember to keep your brand and business names the same across all platforms. Doing so enables social media users to find you easily. This means your current and prospective customers will easily be able to identify you while others will get to learn about your business and your products.

Chapter 3: How to build your brand?

Personal branding is similar to the branding of a product or service. However, in the case of personal branding, this product or service is an individual. Politicians, actors, artists are all known for their unique tastes and style of working, which makes them resonate strongly with a particular section of folks. That is their brand.

Personal Branding is a practice of marketing yourself to a specific audience of people. It is about promoting your skills, ideas & experiences to people who are interested in what you have to offer.

Let us begin with your name. That is your brand. How your appearance distinguishes you from others is your brand design. You have different parents, values, personality, perception, and qualities from others. All these make you unique.

In essence, personal branding is all about being your authentic self.

For example, you might be fantastic at putting outfits and accessories together, which people find attractive. So, with time, you gain followers on social media who appreciate your sense of styling and deem you as a style inspiration. Similarly, you might be great at online gaming, and you share tips and tricks regarding that on social media. Gradually, you gain a following of people who are interested in gaming.

Steps to create And manage your brand:

Knowing Your Strengths

Your strengths are an essential factor in creating your brand. It does not depend on what you think your strengths are, but on what others believe is your secure areas.

Think of people who you feel have a fabulous personal brand. You will observe that these people have complete clarity on what they want in life and who they are at their core. They know their unique selling points and what value they bring to the table. After doing the following exercise, you will join their league too.

Knowing Your Values

Do you have some principles, a code that you use to navigate through life? Those principles form your value system. They determine your moral compass, your personality, attitude, actions, reactions, and so on. Do not confuse them with your profession.

Identifying Your Passion

Have a passion for what you do! That is the biggest secret. It might seem difficult to reconcile the idea of passion and work. But it is not impossible. Clubbing your passion and work will bring you more joy than you can ever imagine. It will keep you inspired and wanting more. That is why influencers are flourishing. They did not take the beaten path or picked a career because many people were making easy money out of it. They picked it because they felt passionate about it and turned it into a viable business model. With passion, you can do that too!

Finding Your Niche

The following exercise will help you understand more about what your niche could be and how you can start to build the foundations of your brand. Be as specific as you can when answering the questions below. You will need this information later down the line.

Who are you? (Write a short paragraph.)

What makes you unique?

List all of your passions (Don't just list things you are "kind of interested in," but the things you are genuinely passionate about.)

What are you good at? (The skills that distinguish you from your friends and family? It can be anything. It might help to think about what people compliment you on and what do you get attention for)

Based on the above information, who could your audience be? (To make it easier, make a list starting with "people who are interested in."

Now you have a list of "niches" that you could become a mega influencer in before we get into the techniques needed to grow a huge following.

Positioning Yourself

Once you are crystal clear about your values, strengths, attributes, niche, and passion, it is time to now position yourself. What does that mean exactly? It means that you establish how you would like others to see you based on your qualities, strengths, values, attributes, and passion. Do not forget – it is all about authenticity. No matter where you work, you must be consistent about who you say you are.

Understanding your competition

Make a list of ten mega influencers in any particular niche or industry. Take a look at how they present their accounts and the kind of content they are posting. What times are they posting? How many times do they update their content? How are they interacting with their followers? How many social media platforms are they present? Is there content the same everywhere, or are they creating and posting different content everywhere? If yes, what are the key differences, and how do they help these influencers?

Carefully select then update your preferred social networks

There are a number of social media accounts out there. You need to choose two or three of the most important based on specific criteria like preference and so on. Once you choose your preferred social media accounts, you should then fully update them, including your business name, address, brands, and then add the content of all kinds. If you have any old accounts that you are no longer using, then close them down or delete them.

Share content regularly

It is advisable to ensure that you share relevant and engaging content with your followers regularly. However, you have to differentiate between sharing engaging and relevant content with spammy posts and overposting. When you post too many times, your followers will consider this to be annoying and spammy. You want to keep your followers engaged and to keep communication lines open. However, oversharing makes you seem tacky and desperate. The ideal situation is posting between 3 and 4 times per week, then responding to comments, queries, and questions about your posts.

Create and curate content widely

You should also create your content or sometimes curate content that you find interesting. Share these with your followers and make it easy for them to share with others or post comments.

Import your contacts

You probably have plenty of contacts on other platforms. Some of the best sources for useful contacts are your email contacts and phone address book. Start with popular locations like Outlook and Gmail then move to your phonebook. You can then check other online platforms like LinkedIn, Facebook, Instagram, and all the others. This way, you will quickly build a decent following in no time. Your followers are likely to have followers of their own. The multiplying factor will mean that you will gain even more followers.

Always keep it positive

Make sure that you avoid being argumentative and stay away from any racial and inflammatory religious comments. Also, choose to be very careful when making political comments because others may disagree with your views, or even worse, take offence to your comments. Should it come down to it, then consider having two different social media accounts where one is personal, and the other is specifically for your business and brand.

Join a couple of groups

Some of the best ways to thrive and grow on social media are through groups. Social media websites such as Facebook and LinkedIn have numerous groups that you can join. To find a relative group, use the search bar on the first page of each social media. Once you join a particular group, you can then engage the members as well as share interesting posts that you come across with your followers.

Benefits of Creating a Personal Brand

It is an excellent way of growing your network

If the efforts you put into your brand go well, you will start gaining followers online, that is, other people who want to keep up with what you have to say on your digital platform profiles. Among those followers, you will find a lot of people who are your current clients and want to keep up with the news, as well as some prospective customers.

It gives more visibility not only to your brand but to yourself as a professional

A personal brand is one more channel to promote your product or service, so it is clear why having one can increase the visibility of what you are selling. When you put yourself out there as the owner of business XYZ, people get to see a part of the brand that they haven't seen before: the person behind it. And a person can be so much more than a business owner! So, having your brand and working on it can get you to a point where you start having access to more (and more diverse) career paths that maybe you would not find with just a business brand.

More Sales

The combination of the four benefits mentioned above, the trust, the connection, the new contacts, and the visibility will increase your product or service exposure, make your audience grow, and, ultimately, translate into the bigger goal: more sales!

KIM MILLUCCI

Chapter 4: Creating a Social Media Marketing Strategy

Evaluate Your Current Marketing Plan

Before you set out to create new goals and plans for your business, it is necessary to go back to the plans you had before you came across this book. If you are working from a clean slate (as in, you are just starting up completely), then go ahead and read through to the next segment. You don't need to take action now, but in the future, you will, as you'll have to evaluate your performance based on the strategies you implemented in the first place. If this is not your first rodeo ride, whip out your pen and notes. It is time to see how far you have come.

- **Objectives:** Your objectives are the compass that leads you to your goals. What are those things you laid out as your objectives? How far have they taken you? Would you say that your current objectives are SMART oriented? Do your best to answer these questions as honestly as possible. Try not to water down failures or overplay your successes and vice versa. You need to be very objective in evaluating your objectives (pun intended).

- **KPIs:** Your key performance indicators are those things that you can use to determine how much growth or sales you have had accurately. For example, your objective may have been to increase sales by 50% by the end of the month. A good KPI would be the number of deliveries that were fulfilled at the end of that time frame. A poor KPI would be the number of followers you got. KPIs give you a metric to help you measure your success. As we have all come to learn, success means different things to different people. In your case, it may be a higher following. For others, it might mean an increased number of clicks and so on.

Create SMART Goals

Now that you have successfully worked out where you are coming from, it is time to work towards where you are going to. Now, there is a possibility that you already have a vision, or at least an idea, of what you want your marketing strategy to look like. Ensure that they are written down so that you can measure them against these SMART goals that I am about to share with you.

Choosing the Right Platform for Your Brand

There are so many social media platforms to utilize for your marketing strategy. While they all serve the same purpose of getting your product and service to the doorstep of your client, not all of them would be able to do that effectively for you. This is because each platform appeals to a particular group of people, and the appeal could be based on gender (Pinterest is a female-dominated platform), age (Facebook has the highest growing number of people above 40) or profession (LinkedIn is mostly utilized by professionals).

Building the Team Behind the Dream

If you are just starting and are limited when it comes to resources, it is okay to start alone. But you have to understand that implementing a social media marketing strategy is more than tweeting or using fancy lingo like growth hacks or algorithms. The core of effective social media strategy is having a workflow and thought process that is centered on the goals that you have established.

Chapter 5: Prioritizing the Top Platform for Your Brand

You are having a hard time deciding which social media platform works best for your business? Read on to determine where you should be spending your budget the most.

Facebook

Facebook is the biggest social media platform and should be approached as such. Whether your audience is most active there or not, a Facebook presence is a definite must. But is the majority of your target audience there?

Facebook is best for B2C businesses, and in some cases, B2B as well. The top industries that thrive from Facebook marketing are:

Fashion

Ecommerce

Real Estate

Health and Wellness

Retail

Sports

Marketing

Auto

Entertainment

News and Information

Did you know that Facebook is considered to be an SEO signal on a local level? That means that search engines check your Facebook profile to give relevant local search results.

Twitter

Twitter is also best for B2C businesses, although some B2Bs may also be at an advantage at this platform. The top industries that benefit from Twitter are:

News and Information

Travel and Hospitality

Retail

Health and Wellness

Telecom

Sports

Finance

Ecommerce

Sports

The most active audience on Twitter is both men and women from 18 to 29 years of age.

Twitter is the perfect spot for customer service. Whenever a customer comes across an issue with a product or service they cannot solve, they Tweet the business hoping to get the solution. Twitter has become the central hub for customers, so make sure to take advantage of his platform and show off your expertise to the world.

Did you know that 93 percent of the people on Twitter who follow SMBs plan to buy products or services from the small and medium-sized businesses that they follow?

Instagram

Instagram is also best for B2C businesses, and if you have got a visual product, then this is probably the best platform for marketing your brand. At first glance, Instagram may seem like nothing more than an app for sharing photos. Still, this platform seriously packs a punch, especially with the younger audience, as 64 percent of the active Instagram profiles are aged from 18 to 29 years. Women are slightly more active on this platform than men, but keep in mind that that's shifting.

The industries that benefit the most from marketing on Instagram are:

Fashion

Travel and Hospitality

Arts and Crafts

Beauty

Food and Beverage

Photography

Event Planning

Health and Wellness

Ecommerce

Auto

Did you know that 80% of all Instagram accounts follow a business? And what's even more impressive is the fact that 72% of them say that they have purchased a product that they saw on Instagram.

Pinterest

Again, best for B2C businesses, Pinterest is a platform that every hobbyist is addicted to. Whether they are planning an event, remodeling their house, or saving yummy recipes, Pinterest is the paradise for everyone who is looking for inspiration and new ideas.

The most active group there are women between 18 and 45 years.

Pinterest is the perfect platform for these industries:

Health and Wellness

Retail

Home and Garden

Beauty

Event Planning

Fashion

Food and Beverage

Travel and Hospitality

Arts and Crafts

Ecommerce

Did you know that a whopping 87 percent of all active pinners have made purchases because of this platform?

LinkedIn

LinkedIn is a platform that is best for both B2B and B2C employment. If you are a business-to-business, then LinkedIn should be the social media platform that you should prioritize.

The most active target group here are both men and women from 25 to 45 years of age.

The top industries that thrive the most on LinkedIn are:

Financial

Manufacturing

Employment

Legal

Education

Marketing

Health and Wellness

Science and Technology

IT

Professional Services

Did you know that the audience on LinkedIn has twice the purchasing power than the average audience on the web?

Another platform that you simply cannot afford not to be present on is YouTube. Although YouTube is undoubtedly different than the previously mentioned ones, it has proven to be of tremendous benefit for businesses of any kind. And while YouTube shouldn't be your primary marketing platform, a strong presence there can be of extraordinary value for your business.

Chapter 6: Twitter Marketing

Twitter is really where the idea for brands being on social media started. It was the first social media network in which people could communicate directly with their favorite brands and became very popular. Twitter was launched in 2006 and has amassed about 330 million active users.

How to Use Your Twitter

Building Your Profile

Building your Twitter profile is a simple task, and it's an excellent place to get used to shaving everything down. The hardest part of any bio on Twitter is the bio. You only have 160 characters, and you have to fit everything you want to say in it. It can be difficult. Your bio has to be memorable, entice followers, and express everything you are. Don't worry about writing the perfect bio: you rarely will get it right on the first try.

Sending Tweets

The general rule of tweets on Twitter is this: the more you tweet, the more followers you will get. Twitter's feed is continually moving and changing because it's so much about being in the now. While they do have a "highlight" feature where when you log into Twitter, the most engaged tweets on your feed show, it quickly returns to that "in the now," always moving feed.

Retweeting

Retweeting is just sharing like Facebook but on Twitter. You can retweet your followers, companies you admire, or things that resonate with you and your brand. You have the option of adding something to the tweet or not. You can even retweet yourself, updating your followers on something that happened earlier, or bringing attention to a special offer that's happening.

Following

On Twitter, people can see who you follow. They might look at your list of people you follow to look for more people to follow or even just to get an idea of what kind of people you want to see on your feed. Follow people you'd want to talk to in real life.

Before you first start following accounts on Twitter, you should try to tweet a few times before you do. That means if you follow someone, and they check out your account, they'll have an idea of what your brand is just by your tweets. Not just an empty black hole because you haven't gotten started yet. You should always have something to show right out of the gate.

Twitter Lists

Twitter lists are one of the least utilized tools on Twitter, and it's a shame considering how useful they are. To explain them in the simplest terms possible, they're just lists of accounts by you, organized by category. You can create lists and follow lists that you like. They have a limit of 5,000 people.

Pinned Tweets

Pinned tweets are tweets that are pinned to the top of your profile. They can be changed every few weeks or every few years. It should be the most important thing you can say about yourself at that very moment. You can tweet about an event or a sale you're having, and then pin it at the top of your profile. That means when someone visits your profile, it will be the first thing they see. If you find value in that, use it.

Hashtags

Hashtags, which is a staple on almost every single social media site in today's world, started on Twitter. It was conceived as a way to keep Twitter users and their tweets in categories. Twitter, as of yet, has not implemented a way to follow hashtags, but it's probably coming especially since Instagram has put it into use.

Overall, Twitter is a powerful platform and easy to use. It's a social media site that is used best along with one or two others and is a great place to engage with your customers directly. You can follow trends and see what you should be talking about right now. Happy tweeting!

Chapter 7: Facebook Marketing

More than one billion people use Facebook daily. This figure has gone on to establish Facebook as the leading platform for social media marketing strategies that are seeking to reach a wider audience. With the tools and features available on the platform, you can open up your business to a broader niche without necessarily sacrificing a lot of money in the process. The platform is updated consistently and so the rules of engagement change from time to time. In this chapter, we are going to look at some of the fundamentals, especially in the areas of advertising rules on Facebook. Beyond that, we are going to look at how you can drive engagement on the Facebook platform and create more awareness about your brand.

Essential Rules of Facebook Advertising

Certain content is blacklisted on Facebook

The category that your business falls underplays a significant role in getting your advert content approved. Adverts that promote illegal practices will not be approved. But it is not just illegal businesses that you need to worry about. There are business categories that may compromise the values that Facebook is trying to promote and may fall under adult content. Ads that contain sexually explicit inferences are not acceptable by Facebook community standards.

Follow the image specifications on Facebook

First of all, the image file must either be a png or jpg, and it must have a minimum of 600 pixels in height and width with a ratio of 9:16 to 16:9. If you are going to add text in your ad image, you have to ensure that it does not exceed 125 characters. If you are going to include a hyperlink in your Facebook adverts, then this will affect the figures I just gave you. The ratios will now become 1.91:1 to 1:1, and the text will come down to a limit of 25 characters. Now, the image itself should in no way promote nudity, sexually suggestive or explicit content, or focus on too much skin. Violent content or material that is considered too sensational might also prevent your ads from getting approved on Facebook. One tricky area that a lot of people don't know about is the inclusion of nonfunctional elements in your image. So, if you are going to include things like a checkbox or a play button that is not clickable, there is a chance that your ad will not be approved.

Keep your writeup focused

When you create an advert on Facebook, it is important to ensure that the copy for the advert is as compelling as possible. However, in trying to create a compelling narrative, you should ensure that you stick to the truth about your brand or company. Be as realistic as possible in the portrayal of your brand; in other words, try not to sell lies. In a bid to convince potential customers to buy into your product or service, do not exaggerate its performances. The copy should also contain information that is relevant to the ad, especially the landing page where you are going to be directing people to.

Follow the targeting guidelines

In trying to find the right audience to market your products, you will need to use the Facebook custom audience tool, which helps you navigate the different demographics on Facebook and decide on the one you feel is the best for you. However, for your advert to be approved for the selected target demography, you have to ensure that it contains information that is relevant to them. Don't be lured by the volume of a particular demographic.

How to Engage Your Customers Through Your Page

Facebook engagement mostly refers to the interaction that people have on your page or post. This could include comments, likes, and shares. Just like the Instagram algorithm, the more engagement you have with your posts, the higher your chances of being featured on the Facebook feed.

Avoid sounding like a sales pitch

Most people that I know do not like the idea of being sold to, and this kind of thinking is also present on digital platforms like your Facebook page. People do not come to your platform because they feel like listening to a marketer reel out the benefits of your product. They come because, more often than not, you possess information that they cannot find anywhere else, or you create content that they can relate with. Anything outside of this will most likely fall on deaf ears—or at the very least, prove to be ineffective as a strategy. Let your focus be on creating content that will appeal to your Facebook demography.

Avoid lengthy content

The vast majority of people who use Facebook access it from their mobile phones, and when scrolling through their news feed, these people spend an average of 1.25 seconds to glance at a post. That is precisely how long you have to get the attention of people on Facebook.

Always include a high image

A picture, they say, is worth a thousand words, and Facebook has taught us that this is so true. A post that has a beautiful image has more chances of attracting the attention of people on Facebook than one that doesn't.

Make them curious

One way to create a buzz in your comment section on Facebook is to ask a question. Questions get Facebook users to engage with your post in the most amazing ways. You can start the headline of your post (no matter lengthy it is) with a simple question.

Don't be stagnant with your strategy. Experiment.

On Facebook, it has been established that videos give you the best engagement across the board. And with this information, it might be tempting to ensure that all the posts you put up on your page are videos. However, because of the updates that are being done on Facebook consistently, it would be very redundant to stick to this strategy simply.

The Facebook Algorithm that Can Change Everything

The Facebook algorithm essentially impacts your presence as a brand of the platform, and while this sounds scary, it doesn't necessarily mean doom and gloom. By taking the time to understand how this algorithm works, you can navigate to those murky waters and utilize the platform to get to the results that you want. The reality is, despite the fears and worries surrounding Facebook's algorithm, Facebook remains the premium marketing platform on social media. Facebook's return on investment remains impressive when compared with other social media platforms. What you need to do is make some adjustments to your content strategy to boost your organic reach on Facebook, and this list will get you started.

Put a lot more effort into your audience targeting on Facebook

One of Facebook's goals is to ensure that when users get on the platform, they enjoy their time there, regardless of how long it is. Now with more than one billion users per day, you can imagine the volume of content that is being thrown at Facebook users. It would make it difficult for them actually to see and access what they are interested in.

Be transparent about your practices

There is a clampdown on misinformation and sensationalistic content on Facebook. People are typically drawn to sensational headlines, and because of this, some devious parties use this as an opportunity to promote content that is violent and sensitive at the same time.

Prioritize the timing of your post

If you do a little research online, you will find that there are specific times that people are most active on Facebook. These times are usually the best times to put out your post or content to drive engagement. The goal of this is to ensure that people are interacting daily with your page.

Make videos the pillar of your marketing strategy

Since we are all about ensuring that our pages have the requisite engagements needed to put us on the feed of our audience, why not utilize the most engaging type of post, which is the video? You can alternate between image posts and any other kind of posts, other than videos, to keep things fresh and different from time to time. But having videos as part of your marketing strategy will increase your chances of driving up engagement.

Push out your content through employees and brand advocates

Apart from Facebook adverts, your reach on the platform is limited to the number of followers that you have. So, if you are trying to grow organically, the post that you put out can only be reached by these people who are already following you. However, if you can get members of your team to share these contents with their network, you can then amplify that reach.

Things You Should Do Right Now on Facebook

Have an interesting brand presence

Your brand presence on Facebook focuses on your brand offering. It gives people more information about you, and if you set it upright, this could become an extended version of your "about you" page. That said, a lot of companies make the mistake of keeping this platform bare.

Personalize your brand

Social media is basically for people to connect with you, and no other platform pushes for this kind of one-on-one interaction than Facebook itself. People want to feel like they are not just talking to a corporate entity or a wall. They want to feel like they are connecting with the human behind the brand. It doesn't matter how antisocial a person is; they still don't want to be serviced by robots.

Become a member of a Facebook group

Facebook is a universe on its own, and Facebook groups are like the LinkedIn version of that universe. In Facebook groups, you can connect with people who have shared interests with you. As a brand, this is fantastic because you are given an entryway that leads directly to the doorstep of the audience you are looking for.

Sync your blog with your Facebook page

There is a powerful possibility that Facebook is not the only social media platform that you are utilizing to promote your brand and business. And so, it only makes sense that you would become exhausted from trying to ensure that posts go up on the different platforms that you are using.

Create a community

It is human nature to want to connect with others. This is why there is a popular saying that "no man is an island." When people come on Facebook, they want to reach out. You can give them what they want by creating a community of people with shared interests. You do this by ensuring that you interact with the people that come on your page not just through the posts that you put out, but you can also comment on the comments that they make.

Chapter 8: YouTube Marketing

Videos are the most engaging form of content on the internet. Articles ask for a lot of concentration from the readers. Pictures are more absorbing, but to communicate something, you have to return to written words. Videos are the most addictive form of content. We all know how time can fly while watching a movie.

As a social media marketer, you can drive a lot of engagement through videos. You can drive traffic to your website or advertise and even sell products directly through videos. The only problem with this great form of content is that it is not that easy to produce valuable videos.

Before you think about getting into videos as a marketing tool, you have to assess whether your content is suited to the video format and whether or not you can consistently produce valuable videos.

Basic Concepts of YouTube

Anyone can sign up on YouTube. Even if you are not a content creator, you can sign up. When you sign up, you automatically create a channel. Channels are where you can post your videos. One account can have multiple channels. A lot of users create different channels for different topics that they want to talk about.

You can create playlists from your videos and other YouTube videos. When you like a video, it is added to an automatically generated playlist for all of your favorite videos. Playlists can help you arrange subtopics in your channel so that viewers can find them easily.

You can edit your videos by using the inbuilt editor. You can add sounds and music to your videos using the free audio library provided by YouTube. You can add closed captions for viewers of different languages. You can add annotations that make the video interactive. For example, you can add a box that links to your website or your product's landing page. In the video, you can encourage people to click on the box. In this way, you can create a call to action buttons on your video and trust me, a video call to action is quite literally a "call" to action and works much better than words typed over a button.

You can also create cards that direct the viewers to some other video or even an outside link such as your website. There are powerful ways to use the YouTube video editor, and you can learn more about it through different videos available on the site.

You can monetize your channel. This is a feature that, once again, makes YouTube unique. You can become a partner with YouTube and earn money through advertisements shown on your videos. If you have a large following, you can earn the right amount of money through YouTube. It's not just a way to market your products but even to make some money!

The analytics provided by YouTube is also extremely powerful. You can get a lot of information about your viewers from YouTube. Use this knowledge to see what demographic is watching your videos and find out if it is your target demographic or not.

The Power of YouTube

- **YouTube is a unique, content creation site.** The videos on YouTube range from a random video blog shot through a low-resolution webcam to massively produced movies and entertainment shows. YouTube is different from all other social networks because when the other networks came along, people found a new dimension to life. These networks created a new niche for themselves in people's lives. But YouTube is the only one that took over the niche that was ruled by television until then.

- **YouTube is also a search engine.** The content creators are in millions, but there are even more people who use the site just for content search and consumption. When you search for something on Google, they show one or two relevant videos related to those keywords. You can also choose to only search for videos. When you do that, you'll find that almost all the videos are on YouTube. Not just that, most people open YouTube and then search within it for "how-to" videos and music videos and movie trailers and so on and so on. This is why being on YouTube is essential if you can create valuable videos related to your niche.

- **Finally, YouTube is also a social network.** The comment sections of YouTube are used more than any other social network. You can get a lot of organic engagement on YouTube. Because of this reason, YouTube comments are also the most honest reflection of the internet. You'll find as many hateful and negative comments as good ones. But if you take the time to manage your comments, you can use it to create incredible value for your customers. You can build a strong fan base that eagerly waits for your new videos.

Success Tips for YouTube

Create valuable content. It doesn't have to be of very high production quality, but it needs to provide value to your audience, either in the form of entertainment or information. Of course, it doesn't mean that it's okay to put out shallow quality videos. At least make sure that the audio quality is excellent. People will tolerate grainy video, but they won't tolerate bad sound.

Create content regularly. The top channels on YouTube publish videos regularly. Some channels publish several videos every day while others publish once a month. It all depends on the type of videos you are making. Most of the time, the more frequently you publish, the better it will be. But you should have a realistic publishing schedule, something you can stick to easily. One video per week, on a fixed day every week, is an excellent frequency to have. It creates expectations from your viewers about new content every week.

Use your creativity to come up with something unique. Remember that 100 hours of video are uploaded every minute on YouTube. What sets your content apart from others? Have a unique selling proposition. Even if you are targeting a very particular niche, try to create something original. How you do this will depend entirely on what products you are trying to market and how creative you are.

Reply to comments and engage with your audience. YouTube has a bad reputation when it comes to comments as there can be a lot of spam or abusive comments, and many popular channels disable comments because it can get tough to manage them properly. There is nothing wrong with disabling comments, but if you have them enabled, then moderate them regularly and reply to genuine people. It is great to see engagement in the comments below your videos. When someone is trolling, you'll see that other viewers will step in to defend you. In a way, the comment section creates brand loyalty in genuine viewers.

Use your brand image for your channel art and link it to your other social network profiles. The cover image on YouTube shows up very differently on mobile and TV. Remember that a lot of people now watch YouTube videos on their television sets, which can connect to the internet. Take some time to create a cover image that looks good in all three formats. When you create the cover, YouTube will show you all three previews. The way to achieve this is to have the essential content of the cover in the center.

Start your videos with a custom animated intro. It gives the impression of a professional YouTube channel, and people will stay with your video for longer. You can even have a 15-second preview of the most exciting parts of the video and then go to the intro so that viewers know what is coming in the video even before the intro. There are plenty of websites such as VideoHive or SmartShoot that allow you to create a professional animated introduction.

End your videos with a call to action. You can simply ask your viewers to like, share, and subscribe to the video. You can also use annotations to create clickable banners on the video that will direct your viewers to your website or a landing page for your product. Asking people to like, share, and subscribe can have a big difference in engagement. Sometimes people might like your videos, but just avoid subscribing because of laziness. When you ask someone to do something, they are more likely to oblige.

Keep SEO in mind and use proper keywords in your video title, description, and tags. Also, remember that the first few lines of the description are the most important because that's what's ordinarily visible on YouTube. To read the complete description, the viewer has to click on "read more," so give them a reason to do so in the first few lines.

Give proper attribution for any copyrighted content that you might have used in your videos in the description. YouTube is big on enforcing copyrights, and if your videos contain scenes from movies or other shows, then make sure to attribute it in the description.

Be ready to spend years on YouTube. Consistent, high-quality content over many years will make your channel accessible. The returns you get will grow exponentially. Only one of your videos has to go viral, and when that happens, all of your previous videos will get a lot of views as well. So, keep creating high-quality content and do it in a way that you enjoy it. If you enjoy it, you can do it for a long time, even if your growth is not satisfactory. Keep at it, and one day it will be.

Chapter 9: Instagram Marketing

Instagram is a visual alternative to Facebook. Instagram works similarly to Facebook, but it's much less wordy. As in just barely. Users upload edited photographs to their profiles and can scroll through their feeds to see the latest updates of their friend's photographs. Instagram has been optimized for the phone and is thus a mobile app. The website is not often used by desktops, which is starkly different from Facebook, which is both easy to use on a desktop or your mobile app. Instagram has been heralded as a creative outlet. While Facebook lets users post status updates about their dinner and work dramas, Instagram is usually drama-free. It has been hailed as the creative cousin of the different social media platforms. With 60% of users logging in daily, Instagram is the second most engaged network after Facebook.

Advertising on Instagram

Sponsored ads appearing in feeds are a recent addition to Instagram. While Facebook features sponsored ads peppered throughout users' feeds, Instagram features the more seamless alternative known as native ads, which means they blend right into the feed. Sponsored ads are the same format and size as users' posts, and therefore are less disruptive and more likely to be viewed by users than other forms of ads. With a range of call to action buttons, such as "Learn more," Download," or "Shop Now," the ads can be very useful in maximizing conversions.

Methods to Promote your Brand on Instagram

1) Host a Giveaway. Giveaways a surefire way to get people to interact with your brand on Instagram. Paired with a clever hashtag and an unbeatable prize, it's a classic way method with a social media twist.

2) Collaborate with an Instagram Influencer. Instagram Influencers are the new marketing tools for word of mouth. Their high numbers of loyal followers appreciate their organic content and take their recommendations on products, travel tips, beauty advice, and anything else to heart. It'll be a surefire way to get your product out to your target market.

3) Hashtag, hashtag, hashtag. While Hashtags are important to use on all platforms, Instagram's search tool is optimized for hashtags. It's important to hashtag relevant topics for your post and to keep it broad and simple. If you are selling a beauty product, keep the tags general, so more viewers will see them, such as "#beauty," "#makeup," "#lookoftheday." Don't forget to add a hashtag of your brand so users can easily find all your related posts with one comment!

4) Share video. Video is the future of visual content, and it's making strides for Instagram. Short clips keep your users engaged, and videos have positive responses.

5) Find and then build on your community. Social media platforms are all about fostering and creating communities of likeminded people. Make sure that you have researched the right groups, accounts, and hashtags that will build your community. Maintaining your share of voice is key in creating a strong digital presence.

6) Interact. Without a doubt, one of the most important factors is to interact with your fan base and beyond. Like, share, and respond to comments, questions, and feedback.

To be more than just a brand to your followers, you have to interact like a friend on Instagram

Tips on how to grow a following on Instagram

Don't be afraid to share experiences, and bring engaging visual content to your brand

Prioritize the experiences over the products, showing what you can do with it, not just the product itself.

Understand your audience and give them everything that they want. Once you know this, then sell based on those factors

Bring creative and different content to your brand

Promote a dedicated hashtag and use it in everything both physically and digitally, such as in receipts, and let people know to use it.

Become creative with hashtags, and don't just use the same ones. C consider trying to branch out on this

When you see conversations, try to talk to people in them, and comment on posts

Get creative with captions, and have them tell stories or share something funny

Use a different bio, and don't just link it back to the website as well.

Remove the tagged photos from your bio that you don't want by choosing edit tags

Approve photo tags before they show so that you can approve the type of content that is seen

Successful Instagram Brands:

Instagram campaigns require visual stimulation. The key for Instagram will be to engage the customer to post their picture and tag or hashtag your brand or slogan to increase visibility further. The campaign has to be captivating and creative. It also has to have plenty of room for individual interpretation and unique styling so that the Instagram fans join the campaign.

Starbucks: The social media star Starbucks hosted a great campaign in 2014 with the hashtag #whitecupcontest, which encouraged Starbucks drinkers to paint their cups and post their creations on Twitter and Instagram. The campaign was a hit and resonated with fans across the board while incorporating their product into the images.

https://www.instagram.com/starbucks/

TOMS: TOMS, the philanthropic shoe company which donates a pair of shoes for every pair you buy, went another route and decided not to show their product for their Instagram campaign #withoutshoes in 2015. Instead, they donated a pair of shoes for every person who uploaded an image. It was surely a bold move, but it encouraged users to participate. It also projected its company values. Officially, it resulted in 296,243 shoes being donated.

https://www.instagram.com/toms/

GoPro: Sure, GoPro has an edge as a camera device in the field of cool photographs. But as far as Instagram goes, GoPro reigns Supreme. With more than 10 million followers, the brand has curated its feed to feature users' photos. From their daily "Photo of the Day" submitted from users to crazy videos showcasing the breathtaking sights from around the world, GoPro has mastered the art of Instagram. The takeaway:

involve your audience. Prizes are offered as rewards. But for most photographers, simply being featured on the highly acclaimed Instagram page would be enough.

https://www.instagram.com/gopro/

Ben & Jerry's: We can't all have the luck of GoPro, whose product seamlessly ties into Instagram. But we can take cues from ice cream dream Ben & Jerry's. As one of the first brands to feature sponsored ads on Instagram, Ben & Jerry's has mastered the art of giving Instagrammers what they love. In terms of content and frequency, the brand has nailed it. With no more than three posts daily, each image is perfectly curated to inspire the viewer on the other end of the phone to get up and buy ice cream. Furthermore, the brand doesn't shy away from political matters and has proudly supported the "Black Lives Matter" movement, further creating a deeper and more meaningful brand image.

https://www.instagram.com/benandjerrys/

Chapter 10: Benefits of Social Media Marketing

Brand Awareness or Product/Service Exposure

Social media sites promote clear communication and new information circulated widely around brands, products, and services. However, these exchanges or transmission of informative messages either enhances positive or emphasize negative word-of-mouth.

Brand exposure ensues when consumers are aware of a certain advertisement, product, or service through exercising, at least, one of their faculties of sight, hearing, smell, taste, or touch, regardless of paying attention to the exposure or not.

Demographic and Geographic Targeted Traffic

With their billions of member users, social media networks truly provide businesses the ideal and convenient avenue for reaching huge target market bases that can even be unlimited in scope. Besides, social media marketing is a very effective means to draw in targeted traffic to your business website or weblog.

Social media enables you to establish or improve brand awareness.

A vast majority of people visit social networking sites like Twitter, Pinterest, and Facebook regularly. Most users get not only social updates from those websites but also news reports and entertainment. They always check their feeds, with many of them having automatic notifications, so they do not miss anything new.

Social media allows you to check where your competitors stand.

Social media is a great way to keep tabs on your competitors. You can join your competitor's Facebook pages. You can follow them on Twitter and other social media accounts. This will allow you to study how they communicate with their customers.

Social media provides a more personalized way of pitching your product.

Social media provides a more personalized approach to promoting or pitching your product. Newspaper ads and television ads seem to be distant and impersonal. Social media is a great venue where you can pitch your products more interactively and humanly. Most people visit social media to get personal with other people. You can get personal with your potential buyers and potential clients by initiating conversations with them. You can also encourage your existing customers to give you feedback so you will know your improvement points.

Social media helps you build client trust and loyalty.

Communicating with your clients in a more personal fashion will make them feel important and secure. It will make them feel valued. This will help them build their trust and confidence in your company and your product. This will also improve your customer feedback, and it will increase the chances of customer recommendations.

Social media helps showcase all your products.

It is much easier and costs less to showcase your services and products with social media. You can post photos of your new products online. You can also post any promotions on products or services that you offer.

Social media make it easier for you to do market research.

Social media will help you listen to what your existing and potential customers say about your products and about the industry that you are currently in. People are more outspoken when they are on social networking sites. They are more honest and critical. This will allow you to discover what your customers think of your product. You can gain a lot of consumer insights and reviews just by taking a look at what people are saying.

You can use social networking sites to strengthen your customer service.

Social networking sites allow you to answer the customer's concerns and questions on time. This will increase customer satisfaction. Social media is also one of the most inexpensive ways to serve your customers.

You can use social networking sites to establish yourself as an expert and showcase your talents.

If you are a life coach, fitness coach, lawyer, or accountant, social networking sites will help you establish yourself as an expert in your field. It is a great way to show off your knowledge and expertise on a certain subject. This will help you get more clients, and it will help build your reputation.

Social media enables you to enhance your relationships and expand your business contacts.

It can do this by helping you reconnect with old friends who can help your business. It can also help generate marketing leads. LinkedIn is great for business networking. You don't only discover people in similar fields, but you also read highly credible posts on important business topics. Join groups and be active on forums. These features are not available to people without accounts on the site, so having one will be important and will also help you establish yourself in your field.

Social media gives you free advertising.

It costs nothing to have a verified account on most social media websites. You can post as many ads and promotions as you want without having to spend a cent. For more advanced marketing, you can do targeted sponsored ads, but this may not be cost-effective for new businesses or those with niche markets.

Lead Generation and Conversion

Based again on the same report from HubSpot, 61% of American marketers have affirmed that their main purpose on why their organization has implemented a social media marketing strategy is to step up their lead generation and conversion activities. To review, leads are your sales prospects or potential customers; conversion denotes the visitors of your website who take desired actions, as purchasing your product or availing your service.

Market Research Insights and Competitor Analyses

Social media and the World Wide Web have transformed the ways of gaining business insights through market research and knowledge about the competition through competitor monitoring analyses completely. Since social media networks are entirely public, you can easily access specific information about your target audience, as well as your business competitors.

Social Customer Service, Consumer Interaction, and Feedbacks

Social media networks also represent broad, valorized, and interactive communication between businesses and their current customers and prospects that frequently foster goodwill and relationships. These sites allow consumers to share their opinions and leave feedback, as well as requests for help and support. As a marketer, you can host a direct conversation with people who either have purchased your products/services or are presently searching for what you have to offer. These individuals could also be your competitors' customers looking out for a better deal, or simply wanting to be aware.

Public Relations and Social Recruitment System of Human Resources

Sales and traffic are not just about the main social media marketing benefits you should consider but also the domains of human resources and public relations. Some of the original movers who espoused the power of social media were public relations specialists.

Social media and public relations are both about establishing, building, and promoting relationships. Public relations specialists use social media every single day to spread a brand's message, to communicate and engage with customers, and to respond quickly to questions or issues.

With social media, professional networking has become much easier, not to mention creating exponential results. Anybody can now link up with people in their fields of expertise or industry, gather the information that helps to advance their professional career, and impress the virtual world of social networks with their professionalism.

Chapter 11: Measuring Your Marketing Success

Here's a question for you: how will you be able to determine if your social media marketing campaign has been a success? Well, there are three methods that you will be able to use to determine how successful your social media marketing strategy has been. Let's find out what those are:

How many people have you reached out to with your marketing campaign?

This one is easy. You simply count how many people you have connected with on each of your social media. This means counting the followers that you have on twitter or your connections on LinkedIn. You can also count the number of likes that your Facebook page posts have, the number of people who have visited your blog, or how many video views or channel subscribers that you have on YouTube.

How many people have directly interacted with you and shared your content?

The number of people who you've reached out to is one thing, but the number of people who have interacted or engaged with you is something else entirely. This one is slightly more difficult to find out but also arguably most important because it determines how well people are responding to you.

For example, how many direct messages have you received on Facebook or Twitter? How many positive ratings have you received for your videos on YouTube? How many questions via comments have you received on your blog posts?

Then, ask yourself how many people have shared your content with others so that you know your content is spreading. Did you receive any retweets on twitter or any shares on Facebook or Linkedin? Has anyone posted any of your videos on Reddit? The list goes on?

How many people have joined your marketing database?

The ultimate goal with social media marketing is to gain new revenue for your business by reaching out to people that you otherwise wouldn't have reached out to. So, ask yourself these questions: how many new online sales have you made? How many phone or email leads do you have? How many new social media followers do you have? How many subscriptions have been made to your blog? And finally, has your overall revenue increased in the time since you began marketing via social media?

You'll never know how successful your actual social media marketing campaign has been unless if you measure it. The best ways to measure it are by the number of people you've reached out to, the number of people who have directly interacted with you and shared your content, and the number of people who have joined your marketing database and the amount of revenue that you have received as a result of these things.

Chapter 12: Why Do People Fail at Social Media Marketing?

When it comes to social media, business owners need to understand that there is a lot to learn. There are several different social media sites, and you must identify perhaps two or three that are most crucial for your campaigns. You will need to learn the rules if you are to be successful and have an advantage over the competition. Unfortunately, small business owners make major mistakes with their social media campaigns; it becomes difficult to make any headway. Here are some reasons why people fail with their social media marketing campaigns:

Anti-social tendencies

The main aim of social media is to provide a platform where people get to dialogue, chat, share, exchange ideas, interact, and communicate. However, some business owners choose not to interact with their followers at all. This is akin to holding a press conference but not taking any questions after that. You need to ensure that you engage your followers and customers on your social media platforms. Do this by answering their questions, responding to their comments, sharing, retweeting, and generally being social.

Key performance indicators are missing

As a business owner, you should learn how to establish measurable goals. This applies to all aspects of your business and not just social media. A lot of marketers out there are not sure what crucial performance indicators to watch out for. They believe likes, retweets, shares, and follows are reliable indicators.

Choosing multiple social media sites to post to.

There is a fine line between posting to Facebook and sharing with other sites and spending all your waking hours updating each social media site. Okay, not such a fine line there is a world of difference. Most of your audience will be on Facebook, but some businesses find their target audience is on Instagram or LinkedIn more often. Sharing a post means some audiences see it multiple times or elect to like your page on the site they use most. It is a better use of your time to share; particularly, when you first get started. You still post to multiple sites, without it taking away from your time.

Not knowing your consumer.

Believe it or not, but some companies are targeting the wrong consumer-based entirely on the social media site they are using. Who do you think uses Instagram and Pinterest? You should know the answer—visual people. People who like visuals, along with words, will not be on Facebook or Twitter as much.

Not posting relevant content.

Relevant content is content that has something to do with what you sell in products or services. If you sell vacuum cleaners, an article on degrading rubber tires for an SUV is not relevant or relatable to your clients.

Not posting, but advertising only.

Launching only ad campaigns will tire out your audience. They will see only that you want to share "products" or "services" without providing value.

Not posting.

You may take the previous two mistakes too far and decide you should not post because you have nothing to say that is relevant or important. It would be a mistake. You need to post. You cannot establish a social media site and not post. It takes thinking outside the box sometimes to find something relevant. The vacuum example would go well with pet dander or pet issues. For instance, an article on why a vacuum is not getting all the pet dander out of the carpet or how to improve your vacuum's ability to pick up pet fur would be relevant.

Using press releases incorrectly can be a huge mistake.

Press releases are not blogs. They are not articles. They are news pieces meant to release something new about your company. If you have nothing new, do not use PR.

Not working on inbound links.

Inbound links need to go to your website and your social media pages. You want people to see your business from Google, Yahoo, Bing, and ads, click on the link and be sent to your website or social media site—depending on the campaign you are working on. Inbound links are traffic. You need traffic.

Not using external links is a mistake.

External links allow someone to follow a link you post and learn something. External links to the competition, a shared post, or relevant content show you are a part of the community and not just spamming your social media site with ads to make sales.

Making grammar mistakes is a mistake for a select few consumers.

People with children, teens, English professors, and teachers are highly critical when there are grammar mistakes in your social media posts. The average person may notice a huge mistake or a consistent mistake. As much as you can, try to avoid making obvious grammar errors in your content. Use online spell checkers and grammar checkers to catch mistakes before you post.

Being inconsistent with your posts, style, and the content will hurt your image and your sales.

Failure to calculate the time and money it takes you to use social media for marketing leads to costly mistakes. You can lose money instead of gaining it if your time is too valuable.

It is easy to get lost in social media. You might see an interesting post, and the next thing you know, you have spent an hour on something else instead of your social media post.

Avoiding social media marketing altogether is a mistake.

Some companies do not think they need it. You are reading this book, so hopefully, you already know it is necessary to reach your clients.

Not using the available tools to track your success with social media campaigns is a mistake.

You need to understand what is going on and whether your site is getting the visibility it needs. You will learn if your posts need to be updated, if you need a professional, or if you are on the wrong site through the use of various social media tools.

Understand the dynamics of different social networks

Sometimes marketers will treat all social media platforms in the same way and use the same approach to market and advertise their products. This is known as a misunderstanding of cultures because each social media is different. Identifying the correct advertising channels is critical for the success of your campaigns. It is just as crucial as identifying where your target market is. For instance, you do not need to get onto social sites like Pinterest or Instagram if you are a web hosting firm. However, if you own a bakery, then Instagram and Pinterest would be ideal for your purposes.

A lack of engaging content

You must provide your followers with quality content that is engaging and relevant. The content can be of any nature ranging from video images to photos to text. The most important aspect is that it is relevant, catchy, memorable, and endearing. Doing this will excite your audience, keep them engaged, and endear them to your business, brand, and products. They will probably leave comments, ask questions, or make queries. When they do, then they should not be ignored. Instead, you should engage them, answer their questions, share and like their comments, and so on. This kind of personal attention is crucial for the survival of your business.

A lack of essential resources

While social media is largely free to use, you still need sufficient resources to keep your campaigns running. A lot of business owners assume that they do not need any resources because these platforms are free of charge. The truth is that you will need some resources to run successful campaigns. For instance, you will need to have a website and probably a blog. You will also need to create content regularly, including videos and photos. With no resources set aside, you will probably fail on your social media marketing efforts. Therefore, before doing anything, you will need to sit down, plan, and strategize for eventual success.

Fear of social media

It may come as a surprise, but a lot of people out there have an unexplained fear of social media sites. This is one of the leading causes of social media failures for businesses. Their fear is mostly that they will post something negative, which will probably hurt their brand. Yet not posting is one of the biggest mistakes that you can ever make.

Chapter 13: Search Engine Optimization & Social Media Marketing

Social media marketing and search engines, such as Google, are inextricably linked through Search Engine Optimization (SEO).

SEO is the process of maximizing the number of visitors to a particular website through ensuring that the website appears higher on the list of results returned by the search engine. As a rule of thumb, the earlier a website or brand appears on the list of the search results on a page – the more visitors it will receive from search engine users. This could, in effect, greatly increase your social media reach.

In effect, improving your social media reach and engagement would organically boost your ranking on search engines, thereby bringing more people to your social media site. Social sharing is key to increasing your ranking for search engines.

Strong content on social media with bold, catchy titles that feature keywords will feed into the engine and amplify the reach of your brand. Google focuses on two main factors when ranking for search queries – relevance and authority. The bottom line for the intersection of SEO and SSM is shareability. Creating and publishing content that has a high potential for becoming viral and being shared is the key to improving your ranking on search engines. Titles, keywords, and phrases that are trending and easily searchable will be of most benefit to increasing visibility of your brand. Titles are limited to 75 characters while descriptions are limited to 160 – so pay special attention to those. Keyword optimization is vital for a link to make its way to the top of the search engine.

Timing is vital, whether it's seasonal or related to a specific event – too early, and the people won't catch it or too late, and the people will already be on to the next.

It should be segmented in that way that your content must address the needs of your segmented audience, one that you know well. Hootsuite and Twitter will allow you to monitor what is currently trending, thereby giving you insight on how to focus your article. Your content should be searchable, which means that keywords need to be referenced and used. Content needs to be snackable, which is not to say it has to be sweet and crunch but rather:

- Well organized
- Sectioned with labeled content

And supported with ample amount of visual aid such as charts, illustrations, gifs, and video.

It will be this type of content that readers will come back to munch on. And finally, your content needs to be shareable. Tags and hashtags are an effective starting point to cover your bases. But more than that, you will need to use your metrics to keep track of your shares and interactions on social media to learn what's working for your users and what needs to be improved.

Chapter 14: How to Build Your Brand's awareness and deliver top customer service

Building your brand is incredibly easy, and you can build brand awareness quite easily. Here, I'll tell you how you can do it, and what you need to do this.

Brand awareness and customer service are incredibly important. Without brand awareness, people won't know where you are, who you are, and why they should care. If you don't know what your brand is and how to get awareness, then good luck.

Building your brand Awareness made easy

When you build your brand, you need to make sure people aware of your band when you're doing this. Some of the best ways to do it are in the tips listed below, which can help you curate and build the best business possible.

First, make sure everything you post is related to the brand. Don't try to go too far out.

Create engaging content that fits with the brand name, being both personable, but also nicely pushing your brand. Don't be salesy, but instead, offer value to your customers, since they're here for that, and not here to listen to you talk about sales. Your goal is to raise visibility at the top of the funnel of sales, and from there, build a better brand for yourself, and others as well. On social media, talking with people and interacting with them is important, and we'll go into networking later on.

When working on building your social media presence, work on just your specific audience, and won't try to market to twenty different audiences. Work to connect with customers directly by speaking to them, and don't be afraid to answer their questions.

When talking to people or seeing replies on tweets, don't leave a question unanswered. You should be able to answer anything that is there at you. Your answers when you respond should be those that involve the values of the brand, and customer-centered content, and from there, create engagement. Engagement is incredibly important for social media marketing, so don't be afraid to use it.

Make sure that you have a logo and brand visuals on your social media channels that are easy for your customers to recognize. The brand and logo should be consistent on all channels, and it will create effective marketing techniques for this.

Now once, you have that, you should work on networking and building contacts, and here are a few tips for doing that easily with social media marketing:

First, find people that are in your brand or field and respond to their social media content. Don't be afraid to talk to them about different topics and build friendships. From three if they follow you, then great, if not, just continue to talk.

If you already have existing contacts, you need to network with them so that you're building better friendships with them, and from there, you can work together to build social media presence.

You should follow experts as well, and learn about what they're doing, and from there, work to build yourself so that you can have a presence. You should also follow experts because often, they have webinars and courses to help you stay current on the latest techniques, so you can curate your social media so that it's simple and effective.

When you do use social media, know where everyone is on the platform, and where you should invest time and service, and work with people that are there that are a part of your brand or can help impact the brand.

When you're networking with others, don't try to copy/paste your answers from others, but be yourself and be authentic and make sure it fits with the brand. Make sure that your social presence is constantly being built, and every network is working towards that presence.

You can also post engaging content, including videos, posts, surveys, contests, and insights, and make it known across social media channels.

Do focus on quality over quantity, and don't try to oversell people or over-tweet to them often. It's annoying, and you should say what you need to say in the clearest way possible.

When you are networking with people, always be nice. Never try to complain to others, but instead be a good person, cause remember, if you complain, people won't want to work with you. Do not try to compare others to others on social media when trying to network. It comes off as incredibly rude on many fronts, so don't do it.

When you network, don't just immediately jump int talking shop, instead talk about business, and work to promote yourself first.

With social media marketing, networking is one of the key tools of the trade, so you should make sure that you use this since it can help you improve your business immensely.

Building Customer Service on social media

Customer service is a very important aspect of social media marketing. It's so important that you need to know how to do it immediately, or your efforts will be in vain.

It isn't just answering complaints either. It's also about answering generalized queries in a reasonable amount of time. Social media marketing has, at its core, building customer service.

It's more than handling complaints, but you need to know how to do that. Two-thirds of social media is used to ask questions and resolve problems, which is a huge number! That's why you must make sure that you answer the questions that you need to.

Basic customer service skills will help you immensely. To start, you must be timely. About threequarters of people who tweet complaints want a response within an hour.

Next, you should know how to find and monitor the conversations that are relevant to your business. That way, you can monitor everything, including keywords across all social media.

You should never wait for complaints either. That is incredibly unprofessional. What you need to do is be proactive in the beginning when you engage followers.

People also love it when brands respond to them. If you've ever seen people excited to all heavens about a brand mentioning them, then you know perfectly well that customers want to hear positive responses from them. Customers that have good experiences with your brand are three times as likely to refer a friend, so being active when it comes to customer service is a big part of it.

You want to connect with consumers to build your brand awareness.

When working with social media customer service, don't use automated tweets all the time. Customer service needs to be personable, and human of course. Never make it robotic or automated. Those representatives reading off those scripts, and scripted messages sound awful. Customer service involves the "real talk" of helping out customers with that issue. It also makes you look more tech-savvy and better with customers.

You need to realize that social media is well, social, and if you give a real, actual response to your customer's needs, then they'll help you, and you'll be able to be freed from the problems. It also pays off in the long run.

When you're helping a customer, you need to make sure that you give real resolutions, and don't just parrot off a response. You should engage with customers in their language and your turf. You should help give a relaxed, unscripted, and real results. This will help show others how much the brand cares, and it gives off that "extra mile" approach and improves impact.

Another important tip for those in social media customer service is to listen. Customers sending private messages often deal with the brushoff tone of most social media. You need to provide real solutions and listen to requests. Don't just dump their queries to help them because it shows that you're listening.

Don't be afraid to say you need to get someone from another department. While it may irritate a customer that they have to wait, it's better to be honest about the problem than just to pretend you know the solution, when in reality, you don't.

When you do give them an answer, always follow-up with them later on, you should try to do it via social media, since the followers will see it, and it'll make it look better as well. I always like to wait about a day or so if you don't get a response right away to find out if everything is all good. That way, it makes you look way better.

Along with that, if a customer has ideas to make the product or service better, ask for it, and if they give it to you, give that feedback to the department and let them know about it. If they feel like the brand is actually hearing their message, they'll stay loyal to them. You can also request reviews at this point in their experience if you feel like you want to go that route, but that's incredibly optional.

Never be afraid to be engaging on social media, and never be afraid to harness your customer service skills to help a customer with their problems. If you're on the ball with this, you'll get traction and success, and it will show in the numbers.

Both networking and customer service are two important tenets of social media, so you should be in the know on both of these and get better with them.

Chapter 15: Simple & Effective Outsourcing to Build Your Social Media Team

If you don't know that much about social media other than the basics or would like to know more information on outsourcing and building a small social media team as part of your business, then a great book that I recommend is "Virtual Freedom" by Chris Ducker. It will introduce you to the world of VA's or Virtual Assistants and is the best book that I have read on new business outsourcing. It's a must-read, and you will discover that it may also be a lot cheaper to use a virtual assistant to manage your social media tasks than you think.

Think about how efficient your local business would be if you had someone that was already experienced with different social media platforms (including the marketing side) to manage and run your campaigns and channels! Your business could grow exponentially because your focus would now be on other parts of your operation rather than putting time and effort into something that may take away from other aspects of your business. This may not be a viable option for everyone, but it may also be something that your business simply can't live without to grow and sustain over time.

Alternative to Using a Virtual Assistant

You may already have someone that is part of your staff, who is an excellent fit for your social media team. If that's the case, then, by all means, do what is best for your business. Be sure this person is learning all the time to staying up to date on the ever-changing world of social media. Remember, this is a technology, and it moves with the lightning appeal.

Another alternative to using a VA is by hiring someone outside of your company that has experience. This could be a very useful option for your business, but it is by far the most expensive. It can work for you if you have the budget to do so and may help your business even if the employee is part-time.

The final alternative is the person that you see in the mirror daily…YOU! If you choose to manage your social media platforms, who's to say that your business can't be a success? My only concern is as your business grows, how long will your business be sustainable, and how will you scale if it's not growing? Just a rhetorical or shall I say a "loaded" question. Why go through the rigors of not focusing on more important things in your business with the exception that you are planning for someone other than yourself to manage your social media efforts? Ultimately, the decision is yours to do what is best for your business.

Chapter 16: Planning Your Social Media Marketing Content

Posting Frequency

Think about how frequently you'll post content on your brand's social media accounts. Is it 3, 4, or 5 times weekly? It's important to determine this from the onset so you can already plot your content posting schedule on your calendar. If you don't, the chances are high that you'll forget to post regularly on your brand's social media accounts, which can significantly affect its ability to engage its audiences consistently. Your posting frequency can also be very helpful in terms of subdividing relatively large chunks of content into smaller ones, i.e., create a series of posts about it. Doing so can make it much easier for you to come up with engaging content.

General Themes

Having a general theme or topic in mind for your brand, product, or service can greatly reduce the need to brainstorm and think about what topics future content will be about. Take, for example, the website https://sunbrightcouple.com. The page's about living a beautiful life even during very challenging situations or seasons. The people behind it have identified several key aspects of life that contribute to one's ability to live a beautiful life regardless: relationships, income, health, and preparing for the future. Knowing their main theme and their subthemes, content planning becomes very easy for them because they already know the kinds of content they'll create or share (other people's content) on their website and Facebook page (facebook.com/sunbrightcouple/), so they no longer have to brainstorm about what content they'll post. All they have to concern themselves with is to create or look for other people's content to feature on their Facebook page.

Automation

Finally, automation solves the challenge of not having "enough time" to post regularly due to busy schedules. There are apps on the Internet that you can use to automatically post predetermined or selected content on your brand's social media accounts at your predetermined times. Through such apps, you can just schedule about an hour every week to create or look for content to post on your brand's social media account for the whole week or month, program it on the app, set it, and forget it. The app will automatically post those content on your brand's social media sites. Examples of these apps are Agora Pulse and Hootsuite.

Chapter 17: Tips and Tricks to Social Media Marketing Success in 2020

Keep all your social media profiles (as well as your website) consistent.

If a user goes on your Facebook and sees you as one type of person, and then goes on your Twitter profile, and sees someone completely different, that will just lead to confusion. It is okay to adapt to the different platforms, as long as you don't lose the essence of who you are in the process.

This consistency also applies to the visuals you use, which should have the same design basis throughout your digital presence; and the usernames you go for, which, in a perfect world, would be the same on every platform. However, that is virtually impossible nowadays because so many people are online, and so many user handles are already taken. Still, try your best to keep them similar.

Share your posts from one platform on other platforms.

For example, whenever you post a video on YouTube, make a post about it on Twitter. That way, a Twitter follower of yours can also become a YouTube subscriber, and your subscriber count goes up. Plus, it is an easy way of continuously feeding your profiles.

Never, ever forget mobile.

With the continuous rise of smartphones and with no one being able to go one single day without data or access to WiFi, not having the mobile world in mind when you work on your digital presence is a sin. So, optimize your website for mobile and make sure it is responsive (i.e., that its layout adapts to the dimensions of all devices, from the biggest computer screen to the smallest phone one). Besides that, use images with the dimensions that each platform suggests and don't include text with small fonts in them. Otherwise, people using their phones will not be able to read it properly.

Engage, engage, engage.

There is no point in working to build the best personal brand in the entire world (wide web) if, in the end, you don't communicate with others and explore opportunities that might come up.

Invest in paid posts.

Everybody is online, yet organic traffic is dead. The way around this problem: sponsored content. There is no need to spend a crazy amount of money or to sponsor every single post you make on every single platform, but thinking strategically and investing on certain posts can make your online following grow exponentially, so make sure to save a bit of your marketing budget to spend on social.

Make sure to include your name and job title on each platform.

For the job title, use your keyword research tool and find the more profitable version of it. Keep an eye on your pages' KPIs. Every platform gives you information on how your posts are doing, and through that, you can understand what works and what doesn't work for your (ideal) audience and then make the necessary adjustments to keep growing.

Chapter 18: Government Regulation for Social media Marketing

When it comes to reasons why there should be some type of government regulation over social media, it isn't hard to come up with viable talking points: Facebook's congressional hearings, Russian trolls, terrorism recruitment farms, questionable content targeted expressly at children; the list goes on and on. Changes to the standards that social media is held to are already being suggested in many places around the world which means there is almost certainly going to be some action taken on the topic in the near future.

As social media is very much a venue for self-expression, this leads to a complicated conversation in the United States and elsewhere where free speech is valued above all else. Likewise, while a wide variety of sanctions against Facebook were proposed, very little ended up coming of its hearings which also indicates that the status quo might persist a while longer. All told, for the time being, it seems the old standard is still in effect when people start talking about regulation the things, they want to regulate typically involve other people.

Negative Effects of Social Media

One of the strongest arguments for regulating social media comes in the form of a morality argument claiming that it may be as important as regulating things like of tobacco and alcohol. While this may sound extreme, the argument at play posits the idea that if left unchecked social media will make it much easier for large corporations to control the overall flow of information as long as they can afford to create the right types of content. This will lead to suppression and choking out of those who are supporting positive issues if they do not have the same amount of capital in their war chest to create their own propaganda as well.

A Curtailed Future

Another reason to oppose regulation comes from the idea of competition and supply and demand. Too much regulation could also serve to discourage innovation in the space as well. The idea here is that if the current suite of social media services isn't doing the trick, then the best solution may well be to start from scratch with a new batch of services that have learned from the mistakes of the past and created something that solves the old problems from the start. On the other hand, if new entrepreneurs are stifled from the start by nothing but red tape and regulation when it comes to building and growing a new business then why would they even bother.

Personal responsibility is key

Finally, there are some people that believe that the issue is one that ultimately boils down to personal responsibility. Effective regulation will need to address the idea that people should be accountable when it comes to determining what sources of information they choose to believe. It is not possible to outlaw gullibility, no matter how many problems this might solve. Likewise, the line between providing a space for free speech and one that intentionally makes fraud easier to accomplish is very thin and hard to determine on anything other than a case by case basis.

While the loudest voices on both sides don't seem all that interested in compromise, there are a few logical paths towards reconciliation that indicate a possible middle ground could hypothetically be reached.

Conclusion

Thank you for your reading this eBook! With the information in this eBook you have now learned how to run a successful and creative social media marketing campaign that is sure to bring your new customers and increase your revenue.

In this eBook, we learned about the huge potential that social media holds for any marketing campaign and why it's vital to your overall success as a business. We also pointed out the challenges that social media marketing presents, in order to give you a more well-rounded view of the subject, but we also came up with proven solutions for overcoming those challenges.

We told you why and how to develop goals for your social media marketing campaign, what three of those primary goals need to be regardless of your brand, business, or social media platform, and then tips for coming up with a plan to ensure that those goals are met.

We also informed you of the most popular or relevant social media platforms for social media marketing so that you can better narrow your selection of social media websites that you plan on utilizing for your campaign.

The overwhelming majority of businesses today, as in over 90% at the very least, are using social media as part of their marketing campaigns. As a result, they've been able to reach out to people within their targeted demographics (or even in new demographics) that they wouldn't have otherwise been able to reach out to. That's why as a business or company owner, making social media one of the focuses of your marketing campaign is an absolute must.

With the information in this ebook, you now know exactly what you need to do and why you need to do it. The result will be your brand spreading across the country if not the world, more and more people coming to your business, and new revenue streaming in that you wouldn't have been able to gain otherwise.

You just need to follow some general rules of etiquette and you'll be fine. Be honest and be human. Spend time in the social media world and stay abreast with the latest trends. Interact with people and build strong communities. Provide real value to your followers and you can never go wrong in social media.

Now that you've read a little bit about social media marketing, you're well on your way to creating the social media platform that you desire. As you can see here, there is a lot that you can utilize, a lot that you can change up in order to bring forth the best experience possible for your branded business.

When you begin enforcing these strategies, your previously quiet or nonexistent audience will start growing and will add spark to life, and you will start seeing significant growth on your influencer.

By using the secrets in this very book, you can grow yourself to the point that YouTube and Instagram want to support your growth as well to ensure that you are both experiencing success from their platform.

Thousands of people have benefitted from these social media marketing tips, and if you're someone who is struggling to build your brand, build your business, and make it work, then look no further. Get the results that you need with this book, and you'll notice the changes immediately.

Good luck!

CPSIA information can be obtained
at www.ICGtesting.com
Printed in the USA
LVHW101024091120
671122LV00012B/549